# The Opening Act

*Melissa Vesna Dasilva*

Copyright © 2023

All Rights Reserved

# Contents

The Opening Act ................................................................. 1
Dedication ........................................................................... 6
Acknowledgments ............................................................... 7
About the Author ................................................................. 8
Scene 1 ............................................................................... 11
Scene 2 ............................................................................... 12
Scene 3 ............................................................................... 13
Scene 4 ............................................................................... 15
Scene 5 ............................................................................... 16
Scene 6 ............................................................................... 17
Scene 7 ............................................................................... 18
Scene 8 ............................................................................... 19
Scene 9 ............................................................................... 20
Scene 10 ............................................................................. 21
Scene 11 ............................................................................. 22
Scene 12 ............................................................................. 23
Scene 13 ............................................................................. 24
Scene 14 ............................................................................. 25
Scene 15 ............................................................................. 26
Scene 16 ............................................................................. 27
Scene 17 ............................................................................. 28
Scene 18 ............................................................................. 29
Scene 19 ............................................................................. 30
Scene 20 ............................................................................. 31
Scene 21 ............................................................................. 32
Scene 22 ............................................................................. 33
Scene 23 ............................................................................. 34
Scene 24 ............................................................................. 35
Scene 25 ............................................................................. 36

| | |
|---|---|
| Scene 27 | 38 |
| Scene 28 | 39 |
| Scene 29 | 40 |
| Scene 30 | 41 |
| Scene 31 | 42 |
| Scene 32 | 43 |
| Scene 33 | 44 |
| Scene 34 | 45 |
| Scene 35 | 46 |
| Scene 36 | 47 |
| Scene 37 | 48 |
| Scene 38 | 49 |
| Scene 39 | 50 |
| Scene 40 | 51 |
| Scene 41 | 53 |
| Scene 42 | 54 |
| Scene 43 | 55 |
| Scene 44 | 56 |
| Scene 45 | 58 |
| Scene 46 | 59 |
| Scene 47 | 60 |
| Scene 48 | 61 |
| Scene 49 | 62 |
| Scene 50 | 63 |
| Scene 51 | 65 |
| Scene 52 | 66 |
| Scene 53 | 68 |
| Scene 54 | 69 |
| Scene 55 | 71 |

Scene 57................................................................73
Scene 58................................................................75
Scene 59................................................................76
Scene 60................................................................77
Scene 61................................................................78
Scene 62................................................................80
Scene 63................................................................81
Scene 64................................................................83
Scene 65................................................................85
Scene 66................................................................86
Scene 67................................................................88
Scene 68................................................................89
Scene 69................................................................91
Scene 70................................................................93
Scene 71................................................................95
Scene 72................................................................96
Scene 73................................................................98
Scene 74..............................................................100
Scene 75..............................................................101
Scene 76..............................................................102
Scene 77..............................................................104
Scene 78..............................................................106
Scene 79..............................................................107
Scene 80..............................................................108

# Dedication

Dedicated to baba
Volim te moja baba
Volim te puno

Croatian translation:
I love you, my grandma
I love you so much

# Acknowledgments

I want to thank my parents for always supporting me. I love you mom and dad, I hope I can keep making you proud.

My baba. I hope you're looking down and smiling. I miss you and I will love you forever. I feel you here with me.

My amazing boyfriend, Ryan, who always encourages me to put my writing out there. His parents Lara and Joe who also encourage me to keep writing. You guys are my second family.

My best friend, Jasmen, supports me unconditionally. Thank you for being the twin sister I never had.

My older brothers Mathew and Anthony. You guys helped shape the person I am today. I am lucky to have such loving older brothers.

My younger brother, Lucas. Thanks for being a pain in my ass.

Aunt Bb. She always believed in my writing and education. My aunt and my second mom, thank you. You aren't blood related, but you are now.

Joanah, my future sister-in-law. Thank you for always being here for me and for loving me like my brothers do. You're the eldest sister I never had. I can't wait to cheer the loudest at yours and Anthony's future wedding!

My publishing team! Thank you for helping me get my name out there. Everyone is so helpful and supportive.

## About the Author

Melissa Dasilva grew up in Brampton, Canada, with her two loving parents and three brothers. Melissa enjoys swimming, reading, writing and travelling. You can often find her playing with her two dogs, three hamsters and two bunnies. Melissa studies Early Childhood Education at Sheridan College and plans to be a kindergarten teacher one day.

The *"setting"* is wherever I wrote the poem.

*Trigger warning*
*This book mentions serious topics like…*

*Depression*
*Anxiety*
*Eating disorders*
*Self-harm*
*Body image*
*& more*

*Please read with caution.*

# Scene 1

*Setting: Pool deck*
*Chapter: Colours*

When I was 3
My favourite colour was pink
Because that was the colour my parents
Chose for my room.
When I was 6
My favourite colour was purple
Because my mom's favourite colour was purple.
When I was 12
My favourite colour was red
Because red was the boy I admired
*Favourite colour*
When I was 16
My favourite colour was yellow
Because yellow resembled happiness,
And happy was something I desperately wanted to be.
Growing up,
I realised that the colours
I chose weren't *my* favourites,
They were other people's favourites,
Or the representation of someone
Who I wanted to be.
From a young age,
I wasn't true to myself.
Now I am 19.
My favourite colour is green
Because it resembles my eyes,
My love for nature,
It resembles the growth of life,
But most of all
My favourite colour is green
Because *I* like it

# Scene 2

*Setting: Pool deck*
*Chapter: Emotion is a strength*

When I was 13
I used to brag that I wasn't
A crier.
*"Crying was for the weak."*
I'd think.
I remember getting smacked in the face
by an overblown basketball at recess.
I held my tears in,
Walked it off.
Showing emotion seemed like a weakness.
I realise that crying is not a weakness,
But a strength.
It takes more strength
To show emotion
Than to hide it
Deep within yourself.

# Scene 3

*Setting: Pool deck*
*Chapter: Social Anxiety is calling*

My body was tired.
I didn't sleep well the night before.
Going to work after the pandemic
Terrified me.
I walked onto the pool deck
With a weak smile.
That's when I got a phone call
From social anxiety.
I tried to ignore it,
But there was no silent button
And the ringtone
Is so goddamn loud.
My co-workers smiled and said hello.
*"They can totally tell that you gained 5 pounds,"*
Social anxiety said.
With a small voice, I say hello back.
*"Your voice cracked. It sounds stupid."*
Social anxiety said.
I walk into the pool office
To see my supervisor.
I'm about to say hello
Until a voice interrupts me,
*"You look so awkward,"*
Social anxiety said.
I cast my eyes down and don't say a word.
I hear co-workers laughing
In the storage room.
I want to laugh with them.
Until I hear…
*"They're laughing at you."*
I sit down on a chair

Trying to look as if I'm not
In an internal screaming match
With social anxiety.
My supervisor walks up to me.
Says to make sure that I have a
Proud and clear voice
When talking to participants.
I say okay.
I stand up.
*"What if your voice cracks?"*
My legs feel wobbly.
*"Everyone will be looking at you."*
My knees give in.
*"Staring at you."*
My head starts to spin.
*"And worst of all… judging you."*
I run into a changeroom wondering.
How my jello legs even work,
Lock myself in,
Close my eyes,
And try taking a breath.
Social anxiety hangs up.
No matter how many people
Tell me to block the caller
Or silence the caller,
I can't.
Social anxiety calls me.

# Scene 4

*Setting: Bedroom*
*Chapter: Question*

But if he
Really loved you,
Wouldn't he be here
To be the one
To comfort
You?

# Scene 5

*Setting: Bedroom*
*Chapter: Uncle Dub*

I miss you.
Despite the mistakes you made in life,
I miss you.
The memory of the horse biting your shoulder,
I miss you.
The way you showed me frogs in the ditch,
I miss you.
The memories of you showing me your birds,
I miss you.
When you took my rock hunting.
It's been three months since you passed.

# Scene 6

*Setting: Bedroom*
*Chapter: My Anxiety*

I wish
I could live just *one* day
Without worrying about
Other people's safety.
*One* day when I don't
Have to make loved ones
Promise that they won't die on me.
*One* day when I don't have to worry
About a loved one dropping dead.
*One* day when the death of a loved one
Doesn't fucking scare the
Shit out of me.

# Scene 7

*Setting: Pool office*
*Chapter: You know who you are*

To the boy
Who bullied me
When I was 14,
Calling me fat
When I was 110 pounds.
Fuck you.

# Scene 8

*Setting: Pool office*
*Chapter: You know who you are 2*

To the girl
Who called me anorexic
When I was 16,
And 110 pounds.
Fuck you.

# Scene 9

*Setting: Pool deck*
*Chapter: You know who you are 3*

To the people
Who makes fun of other people's
Weight.
Other people's weight
Isn't your business.
Their weight
Doesn't determine their worth.
It doesn't matter
If they are small, big, medium,
Whichever…
It
Is
Not
Your
Goddamn
Business.
Leave them alone
And
Fuck you.

# Scene 10

*Setting: Bedroom*
*Chapter: 18 Things I Learned at 18*

1. You shouldn't drive right after getting a G1.
2. You shouldn't listen to insecure boys.
3. You shouldn't listen to insecure girls.
4. Developing a thick skin is necessary.
5. It's okay to cry.
6. It's okay to smile.
7. There is nothing that bunny kisses can't fix.
8. Hold your loved ones close. You never know what the future holds.
9. Many people only show up for the good times.
10. Few people show up for the good and bad times.
11. Not everyone will understand you, but that's okay.
12. There's nothing bad about being *"too hyper"*. You're an adventurous soul.
13. Insecure people hate beautiful and successful people. It has nothing to do with you but everything to do with them.
14. Don't feel bad for calling your mom when you're anxious. She wants to help.
15. Talking to the right therapist is one of the best actions you could take.
16. It's okay to have off days.
17. You should stick up for yourself more often.
18. Always practise self-love. You won't regret it.

# Scene 11

*Setting: Pool deck*
*Chapter: Eating.*

It started when I was 14.
The thought of eating
In the high school cafeteria
Made me nervous.
The thought alone
Was enough to make me
Lay awake at night for hours.
The thought of stuffing my face with food
In front of all those people
Was enough to make me
Stop eating lunch.
They would think that I'm fat.
They would think that I ate like a pig.
Before lunch,
I'd feel my rumbling stomach
And ignore it.
My therapist used to make me
Eat a granola bar
At school,
And I'd hate her for it
Because how dare she embarrass me?
I refused to eat at all.
Even at home.
My therapist told me that if I continued,
I would develop an eating disorder.
What I didn't let her know
Was that I already had.

# Scene 12

*Setting: Pool office*
*Chapter: Shoutout*

Shout out to my therapist
Who listens to my bullshit problems,
But still likes me anyway.
I know it's her job,
But still…
I'm used to people not
Sticking around.
So,
For once in my life
It's nice to have somebody who does:
Even if it's a therapist.

# Scene 13

*Setting: Uber*
*Chapter: Snow*

You remind me of snow.
Not because you like it,
But because you're exactly like it.
Cold.

# Scene 14

*Setting: Apartment*
*Chapter: A Quarter of their life*

The pretty blonde-haired,
Blue-eyed girl in your class
Is actually very insecure.
The quiet girl with glasses
And her head always shoved in a book,
Is actually really loud with her friends.
The star captain of the hockey team
In your school
Is actually trying to get a scholarship,
Because his parents can't afford to
Send him to college.
The boy who cracks the best jokes
Was diagnosed with depression last year.
The smart girl who has her whole
Future planned out
Is actually hanging onto her future stability
For dear life.
You only see these people in school.
You only see a quarter of their life.
So who would you be
If you judged them
From what you only see
A quarter of the time?

# Scene 15

*Setting: Pool office*
*Chapter: After recovery*

Even after recovering,
Even after two years,
I still can't eat
In front of people
I'm not 100%
Comfortable with.
I'll always hide out in
Storage rooms.

# Scene 16

*Setting: Pool deck*
*Chapter: Princess*

I grew up with three brothers,
Loving parents,
And being the only daughter.
They showed me love,
And treated me like a princess.
So there's no way in hell
I'll ever settle for
A partner who refuses
To treat me like a princess
Ever again.

# Scene 17

*Setting: Pool deck*
*Chapter: Hiding*

Do not
EVER
Talk someone down
Or make them feel small.
You never know what they
Are battling.
I once had to hide
An anxiety attack
At work
For 5 hours
And nobody knew.
Not a soul,
Because the only time
I collapsed that day
Was alone
In my room.

# Scene 18

*Setting: Pool office*
*Chapter: Million of Metaphors*

Anxiety crowds my head,
Like angry bees in a
Beehive.
Buzzing, buzzing, buzzing,
Then sting
An anxiety attack…
Or
Anxiety is like a cricket
In your house
At 3 in the morning
When you're trying to sleep.
All you can hear is
The cricket.
You can hear it
But can't see it.
I could describe anxiety
Anyway I want,
I could use any metaphor
But you wouldn't understand.
Not if you don't have anxiety.
There are millions of metaphors
For anxiety,
But you can't truly know it
Without
Feeling it.

# Scene 19

*Setting: Pool office*
*Chapter: Pets*

See?
This is why
I fucking love pets.
They don't care if you're
Fat, skinny,
Tall, short,
Happy, depressed,
Bold, anxious,
Black, white,
Brown, yellow,
Mixed,
Old, young,
Abled, disabled,
Or mentally unstable.
They care whether
You love them or not.
All they want is for
You to love them
As much as they love you.
I mean…
Could you really blame them?
Isn't that what we all want as well?

# Scene 20

*Setting: Bedroom*
*Chapter: When depression hits*

It's the days
When I can't stop overthinking.
It's the days
That I can't stop feeling
Like nobody wants me.
It's the days
When my friends and family
Are sick of me.
It's the days
Where everything hurts.
It's the days
Where my thoughts start to hurt me.
Not just mentally,
But physically too.
It's the days
Where it feels like I'm carrying
Rocks in my heart and lungs,
Getting heavy,
Can't breathe.
It's the days
Where I can't stop crying
For no reason at all.
It's the days
Where I wish I couldn't speak.
It's the days
That I wish I weren't here.
It's the depression days
And today was one of many.

# Scene 21

*Setting: Pool office*
*Chapter: Two Deaths, Two Years*

I don't take death lightly.
When I grieve,
I grieve for two years at least.
It's only after two years
When I can start feeling
Somewhat normal again.
So
Tell me.
How am I supposed to handle
Two deaths
In the span of 2 years?
How am I supposed to heal?

# Scene 22

*Setting: Pool office*
*Chapter: Bitter, broken*

I love you
With all my
Bitter, broken heart.

# Scene 23

*Setting: Pool office*
*Chapter: Recovery*

You came back from the hospital
After your heart surgery.
You had trouble walking and
You looked exactly like Deda.
It scared me at first.
I wanted my healthy Uncle back,
But then I was thinking…
This could have ended so much worse.
You're recovering.
You're still here.
You're still happy,
Therefore I'm happy.
I'm thankful for the successful surgery.
I'm thankful that you're smiling.
Welcome back home Uncle Tom.

# Scene 24

*Setting: Pool office*
*Chapter: Come back*

It hurts to know
That you'll never come back.
I miss you.
Please come back.

# Scene 25

*Setting: Pool office*
*Chapter: Really...*

Is it really
That hard
For some people
To be a decent
Fucking
Person?

# Scene 26

*Setting: Pool office*
*Chapter: Last night*

Last night
I lay awake
Thinking about all the times
I said
*"I love you."*
And meant it,
And thinking about all the times
You said
*"I love you."*
And didn't mean it.

# Scene 27

*Setting: Pool office*
*Chapter: Shy v.s Snotty*

I hate when people think
Shy people are snotty.
Snotty people don't
Want to talk to other people
Because snotty people think that
They're too good for
Anyone else.
Shy people want to
Talk to other people
But can't
Because shy people
Don't think that they're enough
For anyone else.

# Scene 28

*Setting: Pool office*
*Chapter: ?*

I don't even know
What I want anymore.

# Scene 29

*Setting: Pool deck*
*Chapter: Your voice*

Hearing your voice
Over video
Is the most
Heartbreaking
Yet
Beautiful
Sound.

# Scene 30

*Setting: Pool deck*
*Chapter: ?*

I'm grieving
Somebody
Who is
Not even
Dead.

# Scene 31

*Setting: Pool deck*
*Chapter: The little things*

It's funny
When someone has been
Gone for a while,
But the little things
Still remind you of them
In your everyday life.
Like how he used to buy
Bird food for the wild birds,
Or have a huge bucket
Of rocket lollipops to give
To my brothers and I,
Or how he used to love to see
The mother bird lay her eggs,
Or how he always used to wear
Trousers with a button-up shirt.
It's the little things.

# Scene 32

*Setting: Pool deck*
*Chapter: I'm sorry*

Some people say
*"I'm sorry."*
And mean it.
Some people say
*"I'm sorry."*
And only say it
Because they got caught.
Now,
The difficult part
Of that
Is not knowing the difference.
How do we
Truly know if
Someone means it
Or not?

# Scene 33

*Setting: Pool office*
*Chapter: 8:27 AM*

I wish it could
Have been different.
I wish
I never met you.

# Scene 34

*Setting: Pool deck*
*Chapter: I knew he didn't love me when...*

I knew he didn't love me when
He didn't want to
Take 5 seconds
Out of his day
To read the poem
Or story
That I wrote
For him.

# Scene 35

*Setting: Pool deck*
*Chapter: The list*

Things that embarrass me:
- Talking
- Eating
- Walking
- Running
- Sneezing
- Stuttering
- Coughing
- Falling
- Hiccups
- Laughing
- Drinking
- Jogging
- Clapping
- Snapping
- Walking through crowds
- Yelling
- Getting yelled at
- Making any noise
- Drawing any sort of attention to myself
- Going up in front of many people

And many more.
Is this normal?

# Scene 36

*Setting: Bedroom*
*Chapter: Bitter*

So
I take a shot of poison
Because the bitter taste
Is better than
The bitter thought
And reality
That you're not
Coming back.

# Scene 37

*Setting: Bedroom*
*Chapter: Control*

I starve myself for control,
Because control is something that
I don't have much of it.
I can't control that they left,
So instead, I control
The things passing by my lips.
I can't control my anxiety,
So I control the empty way
My stomach feels.
I can't control the fact
That he hates me,
So I shave the fat away
From my bones.
Starvation is my power.
And the only thing I can direct.

# Scene 38

*Setting: Facility room 2*
*Chapter: Simply shrink*

If my body could talk,
It would not.
My body would scream,
Break my bones,
Shrink my skin until it
Feels like a skin-tight
Leather jacket.
Drain my blood,
Bite my tongue.
I would simply shrink.

# Scene 39

*Setting: Pool deck*
*Chapter: What I Want to be*

You always get those questions
When you're younger.
An adult crouching to look
At you face-to-face.
*"What do you want to be when you grow up?"*
5 year-old me would say,
*"A princess."*
7 year-old me would say,
*"A teacher."*
12-year-old me would say,
*"A veterinarian."*
15-year-old me would say,
*"An author."*
Now, 19-year-old me says,
*"Happy, and to stay happy."*

# Scene 40

*Setting: Pool deck*
*Chapter: The moment that stuck with me*

I remember when I had just turned 15.
I was sitting on my boyfriend's living room couch.
(Now ex).
We were talking to his mother
And laughing.
His little brother walked down the stairs
Complaining about a girl in his class.
She got better than him on a test,
And he was annoyed.
My boyfriend's mother sat the little brother down,
Looked at him in the eye,
Smirked,
And said,
*"If she annoys you again, call her fat, ugly, or both. It's something that she will hold with her for the rest of her life."*
Both her sons laughed
While I sat there in shock.
How could a women
Purposely turn against her own gender?
Before his little brother spoke,
I did.
*"That isn't nice,"*
I responded,
To which the mother laughed.
*"He's a boy. He doesn't have to be nice."*
It shames me that I was
Silent after that,
More so that I continued dating my boyfriend.
From that moment,
I should have known we

Wouldn't have worked out,
But that is beside the point.
The point is that sexism still
Exists.
Sometimes it may be someone from
Our own gender.
Why is it that
The greatest insult
People could give to women
Is about her being
Fat, ugly, or both?
Why is it that people
Only see us as a body,
And not our smart minds?
That moment stuck with me.

# Scene 41

*Setting: Pool deck*
*Chapter: 7 years*

They say that
Your body replaces
Itself after 7 years.
Now,
I don't know if that's true or not
But
It's been 4 years.
3 more years left
And I will be pure.
100% nothing left
Of you
On me.

# Scene 42

*Setting: Pool deck*
*Chapter: Sensitive*

When I was younger
(And even now)
People liked to call me
Sensitive
As an insult
To justify hurting me.
I've got it so embedded
Into my brain
That when someone hurts me,
I blame myself.
They could set fire
To me with flint and steel,
And I'd think it's my fault
Because I have
Tears of gasoline.

# Scene 43

*Setting: Pool deck*
*Chapter: Some days*

Some days I fall asleep
Content with his voice
On my phone speaker.
Some days I fall asleep
From the drowsiness of my
Clonazepam.
Some days I wake up
To butterflies in my stomach.
Some days I wake up
To bats in my stomach.
Some days
I'm out and about,
Enjoying the soft air
On my pale skin.
Some days I listen to
Niall Horan on repeat in bed,
Stuck on a clock that won't move,
Won't budge.
Some days all I want
To do is move.
Some days all I want
Is to stay still.
Some days living
Feels like a gift.
Some days living
Feels like a chore.
Some days
All I can do is breathe
And that'll be enough.

# Scene 44

*Setting: Pool deck*
*Chapter: Crystals*

I'm sitting crossed-legged on my bed
Listening to music.
The next song that plays:
Crystals by monsters and man.
I immediately close my eyes.
I could smell the fresh lake.
I could feel the grass tickling my toes,
As if I teleported to that
Summer in 2017.
I could hear the laughter of my camp friends.
I feel myself smiling.
I can feel the tears rolling down my cheeks
From the first time I ever told
Anybody about the inside
Of my soul…
Because those friends were
The first friends that made me
Feel loved,
Made me feel like I can
Be myself,
And they'd still love me no matter what.
I could still taste the grilled cheese.
How crispy the edges were.
That was my first time ever
Eating grilled cheese.
I could still feel the
Green string on my wrist from
When I passed the lake swim test.
I could see the wet lake
Droplets on my skin from
My friends splashing me.

I could still feel my friends
Soft skin as I held her hand while
She finished telling us about
Her dark past.
The song finishes
And my eyes fly open.
I'm not 14.
I'm not at camp,
And I'm not beside my friends.
I'm hundreds of miles away,
In a whole different province
And city.
The friends that once held
My deepest secrets
Contact me through a
*"Happy birthday"*
Once a year.
I'm now 19
With tears streaking my cheeks
While sitting crossed-legged on my bed.
Not sad ones,
Not happy ones,
But bittersweet tears…
Because at least I experienced that
Kind of friendship,
And who says that
I can't again
But in my own city this time?

# Scene 45

*Setting: Pool deck*
*Chapter: Advice to My 14-year-old Self*

We're young, and we're fucked. We make mistakes. We fill the air with fruit-flavored smoke. We drink until our liver cries. We smoke until our lungs are charcoal. We get higher than a plane. Perhaps you think about your ex even though that shit is in the past. Do you really think that out of millions of people in the world, one person who can't treat you right is the only soul who speaks to you? Think again. Travel. Money comes back, but experience and time don't. You're here one day and dead the next. Do you believe in a God or not? It doesn't matter because the most important person you have to believe in is yourself. Fall in love. It will either work out or hurt. As long as you feel something, that's all that matters. Stop lying in bed all day. Do something because as you get older, you're going to regret not doing anything when you had the opportunity to do it. Go on that roller coaster. Go jump off that plane with a parachute. We aren't meant to wake up, take Zoloft, then go to sleep again. When your hair is grey, and you sit your wrinkly ass down on a chair, you should have stories to tell your grandkids or younger generation. Speaking of getting old, go to your grandparents and learn about your history and culture. Treasure them because they are a gift. They are only with you for so long before they go. Learn from their stories and mistakes. Go and make your mark on this world. The biggest mistake you could make is doing nothing at all. Perhaps you will learn from this poem, perhaps you won't. You will learn one day, hopefully, sooner rather than later, because this is a poem that I should have read when I was 14.

# Scene 46

*Setting: Pool deck*
*Chapter: Part 1*

He wanted me first/ he was nice/ he laughed at my jokes/ he made me feel liked/ he asked me out/ I said no/ I was scared/ I was innocent/ 14/ never had a boyfriend/ he guilt-tripped me/ mistaken my friendliness for flirting/ I felt terrible/ I said yes/ told him that I changed my mind/ he was happy /I didn't know how to feel/ young relationships don't last long/ right?/ he texted me when I felt down/ called when I asked him to/ held my hand/ made me think that I made the right decision to say yes/ I started to get attached/ he pulled away/ I didn't know what to do/ I was not experienced/ what do I do?/ I didn't have friends/ he isolated me/ he left his tablet in his locker/ I took a look/ I saw pictures/ nudes/ of other girls our age/ I cried/ he caught me/ he yelled at me/ called me insecure/ he apologized/ I went home/ he called/ he apologized/ I accepted/ I wanted to feel liked/ a week later/ I caught him/ taking a picture/ of a girl's butt/ she was clueless/ I tried to tell her/ I couldn't speak/ why was I such a pushover?/ I didn't want to be this way/ the next day/ he told me that he loved me/ I didn't respond.

# Scene 47

*Setting: Pool deck*
*Chapter: Part 2*

Don't leave me/ he pleaded/ I was weak/ he said he loved me/ did I love him?/ no/ I loved the feeling of feeling needed/ I need you/ you're not like other girls/ he apologized/ I accepted/ I was stupid/ I was scared/ His friends teased him/ said he has a bunch of hoes/ in front of me/ they were indirectly but directly telling me/ his friends laughed/ he laughed and agreed/ his friends thought that I was pathetic/ I guess I sort of was/ I was too innocent/ I gave up on trying to break it off/ I was desperate/ It got to a point/ where I regularly saw/ videos of his girl friend/ twerking for him/ I cried/ he didn't care/ I was depressed/ he didn't believe in depression/ this is my fault/ I did it to myself/ he backed me in a corner/ kissed me/ I said no/ I hated it/ I said no/ stop/ no/ no/ no/ please stop/ he didn't listen/ it's my fault that he didn't listen/ how could anyone take me seriously?/ I'm pathetic/ I let him walk all over me/ too many times/ he was used to it/ he touched me/ covered my mouth/ I couldn't scream/ I was gone too far/ my body didn't feel like mine/ I've never been so excited for the school year to end/ I didn't have to see him every day/ I blocked him/ left no trace/ I was truly alone/ but it felt better than being with him.

# Scene 48

*Setting: Pool deck*
*Chapter: Flaws*

Okay, so maybe I self-sabotage too much/ without meaning to/ I brush my hair too much/ I cry too much/ I hate the way I look/ I feel fat/ I feel ugly/ I don't wear my glasses even though I can't see shit/ Being an ounce prettier seems far more important than my own needs/ I'm bad at math/ my hair is too stringy/ a mix of brown and blonde/ dirty blonde/ here comes the dirty blonde jokes/ I'm a mix of sad and confused.

# Scene 49

*Setting: Pool deck*
*Chapter: Introvert*

I always preferred
To be
In my own little world
Anyway.

# Scene 50

*Setting: Pool deck*
*Chapter: Anxiety leaves a voicemail*

*Beep...*
Hey! It's me, Anxiety. Remember the time you ran into the pole when you were 13? Remember-
*Delete voicemail.*
*Incoming voicemail...*
Hey, Anxiety again. Make sure that you act as normal as possible when other people are around. You're a little weird… so don't scare them off. Also-
*Delete voicemail.*
*Incoming voicemail...*
It's Anxiety. You start college in person next week, but are you sure you want to go? You may get lost in those long hallways, and you'll have to speak to people. You're going to feel out of place. You're-
*Delete voicemail.*
*Incoming voicemail...*
Hey, it's- you guessed it- Anxiety speaking. This world is going to shambles. Do you think another world war will happen? Do you think you'll get drafted? Do you think another pandemic will happen? Do you think-
*Delete voicemail.*
*Incoming voicemail...*
Anxiety speaking. Did you check on your loved ones today? They could die at any second, and you won't know until later-
*Delete voicemail.*
*Incoming voicemail...*
Hey, it's Anxiety. If you keep ignoring my calls and deleting my voicemails, you'll regret it. Instead of anxiety, call me a lifesaver. I help you think about the what-ifs, so that you're prepared! Instead of anxiety, call me future

predictor because I will warn you about all the possible future events. Don't ignore me. I will keep calling. I WILL SHOUT UNTIL MY VOICE IS RAW. You can try writing until your hands cramp, colour until your knuckles are white, or read until you physically can't. No matter what you do, I'll make sure you hear my message, loud and clear. Now think about everything I said. I can't wait to talk to you soon.
*Beep...*

# Scene 51

*Setting: Pool deck*
*Chapter: Love is a drug*

Out of all the drugs
That could harm you,
Make you change,
Kill you…
I think love
Is the most
Addictive,
Dangerous
One of them all.

# Scene 52

*Setting: Pool deck*
*Chapter: #aesthetic*

Do you know
*"That girl"*?
The one who posts her
Green smoothies on Instagram,
And her morning routine
On TikTok?
*"That girl"* who wakes up
At 5 in the morning
With her white and perfectly polished,
Fluffy robe?
She eats her perfectly healthy
Breakfast before getting into
Her BMW to drive to the gym.
*"That girl"* who works at her
Oddly clean apartment,
On her expensive laptop,
With perfectly clean and
Manicured nails.
She can afford 10 dollar coffee,
And everything in her life fits
Her shade aesthetic.
From the clothes she wears,
To her water bottle.
Her hair is never out of place,
And at the end of the video
She claims that she had
*"Such an unproductive day!"*
Making us regular people
Feel shitty about our lives.
Let me tell you something:
That is toxic.

She is acting,
Because there is no such thing as
*"That girl"*.
Her whole *"daily routine."*
Is an act to make herself
Look perfect.
Let me tell you another thing:
I wake up with eye crust and tangles.
I trip over clothes lying on
My bedroom floor.
I press the snooze button 4 times.
I grab a granola bar and
Call it breakfast.
I don't need a fancy car,
Nor 10-dollar coffee.
I apply deodorant in the car
Because I forgot this morning.
Damn, I don't even think
My clothes match.
I'm just proud that I at least
Got out of bed this morning,
And you should be proud too.
I'm imperfect, and that's okay.
Don't pretend to be perfect to make
Yourself look good.
When the camera is off,
You know that your morning routine
Will look a lot more different.
Stop trying to be "that girl"
And be your own girl instead.
It's more real.
It's more beautiful.

# Scene 53

*Setting: Pool deck*
*Chapter: My first heartbreak*

I was 15 years old when my dad walked into the house and told me the truth. It was an 8 month relationship, but we've been best friends for much longer. He was never the perfect boyfriend, nor will he ever be, but I was just looking for a human. Not perfect. He did and said a lot of shitty things, but I loved him nonetheless. You don't get to pick and choose who you love. It just happens even when you're not looking for it. He was my first real, mature boyfriend. The boy I brought home to my parents: I consider that real.

So, when my dad walked into the house that day, I was sitting nervously on the couch. My dad looked angry, and my heart dropped. It didn't look good. He sat me down and told me the news. I cried. It felt like a brick was being hurled toward my chest. What's the point in having a ribcage if it doesn't actually protect the heart? His true colors were being shown. It felt like I didn't know him. He was playing an act for all this time but now? The play is over.

My mom hugged me while I wailed. I know it hurt her to see me in so much pain. It was something that she couldn't protect me from, but she stood by my side, and that was enough.

One day when I have a daughter, I want to do the same. I know I can't protect her from heartbreak and selfish boys or girls, but when the clouds turn grey, and it starts to pour... she at least knows that she can come into my home that is called my arms.

# Scene 54

*Setting: Pool deck*
*Chapter: My graduation quote*

When I was choosing my
High school graduation quote
In 2020,
I was forced to look back into
The past 4 years.
I didn't like high school.
It was more painful than fun.
I got through it by listening
To Niall Horan on repeat,
Shoving my earbuds in my ears,
And shuffling down the hallway.
I was quite the fan girl back then…
Still am…
I was trying to find myself.
Trying to not have a panic attack
In 11th grade gym.
I had one good friend,
Everyone else pretty much sucked.
So,
When it came to picking out a
Grad quote…
The aesthetic girls picked
Inspirational quotes,
The funny kids picked
Witty quotes,
The depressed kids picked
Show inside jokes,
The sexist, racist bros picked
Rapper quotes,
The kids who wanted to be different
Had no quote at all.

Maybe I was overthinking this
Whole grad quote,
But it felt like I had to
Pick one that sums up
What I learned.
At the end of the year
I decided to pick…
*"Why would you wanna play someone else/I love you best when you're just yourself."*
By none-other-than
Niall Horan.

# Scene 55

*Setting: Pool deck*
*Chapter: Depression shows in many ways*

Depression is more
Than not wanting to get out of bed,
Or feeling hopeless,
Or crying until you can't breathe,
Or wanting to die.
It's digging your nails into your skin,
Not wanting to pee even when
You really have to,
Not being able to cry or show
Any emotion at all.
It's also getting up to go
To work or school,
And faking a smile on your face.
Depression isn't just one symptom.
It shows in all different
Kinds of ways.

# Scene 56

*Setting: Hockey arena*
*Chapter: Dear Anxiety,*

Most times, you come fast.
I'll be sitting in my bed,
Thinking…
Then you come along.
It's like a painful rush,
Because I wasn't expecting it.
Sometimes it's a slow and painful attack.
I'd feel it coming from a mile away.
I'd get anxious about being anxious.
Then
I'd get anxious about not being able
To handle my anxiety.
It slowly gets worse
Until a panic attack comes.
Like a slow and painful death.
But what is worse?
A fast panic attack or a slow one?
The answer to that question is
None of the above,
But if you have anxiety
You know that none of the above
Is not an option,
And that option is the most painful
Part of anxiety.
You're here to stay,
Aren't you?

# Scene 57

*Setting: Pool deck*
*Chapter: I'm not fucking perfect*

I am the shy and quiet girl
Who brings her purple notebook around
To write poems.
I am the girl who sits
Around unbothered,
With her nose dug deep into a novel.
The girl, the parents, point out
To their daughters and say,
*"You ought to be that girl's friend. She seems like a good girl."*
Now,
Am I a good girl?
Maybe.
I've never given my parents a hard time.
Well…
Sometimes,
But not all the time.
What people don't understand is
Just because I'm quiet and shy,
Doesn't mean that I'm not fucked up…
Because I am fucked up.
I have panic attacks, and to prevent them
I have to take a pill which makes me
Look like a drug addict for 3 days straight.
I have bipolar disorder, and it's hard for
People to deal with me because of it.
I once took an eddie because my anxiety was
Over the roof.
I tripped like crazy and learned that eddies
Don't help.
I distance myself from people.

I take sleeping pills that aren't prescribed
Just so I can fall asleep.
I drink when I'm upset,
And I'm just a fucking mess.
So
When people find out that I'm more
Than the quiet girl,
They place me as this horrible human.
I'm not fucking perfect.

# Scene 58

*Setting: Pool deck*
*Chapter: Dear Self-love,*

I hope we find
Our way
To each other
Someday.

# Scene 59

*Setting: Pool deck*
*Chapter: 4 years ago*

If you told me 4 years ago
That now
I'd be working and going into
College without having an anxiety attack,
I wouldn't have fucking believed you.

# Scene 60

*Setting: Pool deck*
*Chapter: Poetry*

Everyone always says that
Poetry is beautiful.
Although that statement may be true
For some poetry,
It doesn't speak for all poetry...
At least not mine.
Most of mine are disturbing,
Raw, foul,
But most importantly...
Real.
And not all real things
Are pretty.

# Scene 61

*Setting: J310 Sheridan*
*Chapter: Hurt people, hurt people*

"Hurt people, hurt people.
Fuck that.
Although that statement is unfortunately true,
I can't comprehend it because...
I've been hurt.
I've gone through shit.
I've had breakdowns.
I've felt depressed.
I've felt numb.
I've felt pure hatred for myself.
I've felt anxious.
I've felt those feelings too.
The difference between us
Is that you feel shitty,
So you want others to feel shitty,
Even the innocent.
I feel shitty.
I know how low it gets
So I'd never want anyone else
To feel that way.
All because I know how much
It hurts,
How much it affects.
The self-pitying hurt people,
Hurt people.
The real hurt people who knows how
Low the low could get,
Don't ever want to make
Anyone else experience that feeling.
Self-pitying hurt person...
Be better.

Not just to yourself but to other people.
To the genuine hurt people…
Props to you.
I hope you heal.
I love you.
I wish you the best.

# Scene 62

*Setting: Pool deck*
*Chapter: Toxic*

One day
If my anxiety were
To ever vanish,
I wonder how I would feel.
I'd love the nagging,
Judgemental,
And scared voice
Is gone…
But I would somehow
Miss that voice
Because I'd feel lonely.
…
This is why I think that
I stayed in toxic relationships
And friendships.
I'd do anything…
Even break myself
So that I wouldn't be lonely.
That's not anyone's fault but mine.

# Scene 63

*Setting: Bedroom*
*Chapter: The key to life is feeling*

A lot of people think
That they're bigger and superior
When they say
They feel numb.
They don't feel emotions.
Then they create this
*"Cool aesthetic"*
Of feeling numb.
To me,
Feeling numb is, weak and
Not strong.
You can tell me,
*"Melissa, you just haven't gotten to that point in depression."*
But I did,
And I was the weakest when I was numb.
The most strong thing
You can do
Is feel.
Any emotion,
As long as you feel.
Being numb
Is not a good thing.
Being a numb asshole and being a jerk
To everyone in your life, because you're numb
Isn't cool.
Not feeling bad after hurting people
In your life
Is not an aesthetic.
I've gotten to the point where
I felt everything and

I felt nothing.
I'd choose to feel instead of not,
Because this is life.
You have to be sad or
Mad or
Anxious or
Sad or
Any type of negative emotion
To be able to appreciate
Being happy.
Just like you have to go through
A rainstorm to
Appreciate the rainbow at the
End of it.
If life was always happy,
Then is it really happy?
The key to life
Is being able to feel.
If we always see rainbows,
What would be so special about it?
Think about that.

# Scene 64

*Setting: Pool deck*
*Chapter: Pro-choice*

Hate me, if you will, for saying this,
But I'm saying it.
If you haven't guessed already,
I'm pro-choice.
That means that
It's not any of my business or choice
On what women do with their bodies.
This is for the males who are pro-life:
What makes you think that you have a say
In what women do with their bodies?
In reality,
It's not your body
So it's not your choice.
If you argue that there
Is a living being inside her body,
Then why don't men pay child support
Right when the fetus is in her stomach?
Why only start paying after
The child is born?
I know what you're going to say,
I could hear it from a mile away.
*"Women only care about a man's money."*
Men only care about control,
Which is why you're pro-life in the first place.
If you're so pro-life,
Then why aren't you vegan?
Meat is an animal.
That animal once had a life that got taken away
To become meat,
Is it not?
But no,

That shouldn't count.
Any point a woman makes
Doesn't count as a pro-life male.
So this is what I have to say to
Pro-life men.
Fuck your control,
This isn't your body.
I will get an abortion if I want to
And you will have no say in it.
Fuck your control.

# Scene 65

*Setting: Pool deck*
*Chapter: Why, mother nature?*

It's March 15th
And there is snow outside
With people yelling,
*"Mother nature, why? Why is it still snowing in March? We want spring."*
I wonder if
That's how the inside of my head feels.
*"Melissa, why? Why is it still dark after 7 years? We want light!"*

# Scene 66

*Setting: Pool bench*
*Chapter: Don't get it twisted*

99.9% of the time
I feel like I'm undateable.
I think that I'm too messy and
Too complicated
For someone to fully
Understand.
I mean,
How are they supposed to understand
What's going on in my head
If I don't even understand?
I'm made out of
Blood, skin, and
Heartache.
I'm bipolar.
I'm depressed.
I'm anxious.
I can't talk without overthinking.
I mean,
Who wants somebody like that?
I'm boring.
All I do is read, write, go to school, work,
And take care of my pets.
No guy wants to date someone
With a bland personality like mine.
It's not like I make up for
The lack of personality with my looks.
I've got a baby face.
I'm 19 and looking 13.
I'm flat in all the places that need fat,
And fat in all the places that need flat.
Damn,

I can't even do my eyeliner right
And I love eyeliner!
Most people think that I'm
Mysterious at first glance…
Until they find out that I can't even
Do a normal human thing like
Eat without feeling guilty,
Or throwing it all up.
This poem isn't supposed to be about me
Trashing myself,
But supposed to be a poem on how
Sick and tired I am of guys
Thinking that I'm quiet and
Mysterious poet that they want to date…
Until they realize that I have flaws and
Bleed through my poetry.
Then they leave,
Making me more shattered than the last.
The most I could do was be a decent poet.

# Scene 67

*Setting: Pool office*
*Chapter: Scene? Happy?*

Is this the part
Where the main character
Heals from her trauma?
Her heartache?
Maybe overcome her fears?
Is this the scene where
She finds her true self
After being lost for
Days/months/years?
Do you know the scene I'm
Talking about?
Where she is happy and
Her life is mostly
Back to normal?
Is this it?
"No."
The author says,
*"You still have a long way to go,"*
Darling.
I know it's hard,
But the end is always sweeter
When you've been waiting and
Looking forward to it."

# Scene 68

*Setting: Sheridan*
*Chapter: Conversation with my therapist*

It goes something like this:
*Melissa, how are you?*
If I were good, I wouldn't be here.
*Melissa...*
Sorry, I'm fine.
*Are you anxious?*
No.
*I hear you picking at your nails.*
That's not me.
...
...
Sorry, okay, that's me.
*Any events leading up to you before being anxious?*
People.
*What about people?*
They suck.
*Elaborate.*
They make me nervous.
*Are you nervous right now?*
No, I'm extremely happy. Practically dancing on my rooftop.
*Your sarcasm is a little too much today. That's how I know you're nervous.*
I prefer to call it humor.
*Whatever you want to call it, that's fine.*
Okay.
...
...
Guess what I got at the mall today?
*So, you're anxious because you went to the mall today. Tell me about that if you're okay to do so.*

That is not the point. The point is that I bought a skirt.
*I'm sure that you being anxious at the mall is more of "the point" than buying a skirt.*
I guess, but do you know what color the skirt is?
*The point of therapy is to talk about the issue.*
The skirt is the issue.
*Oh? Elaborate.*
They didn't have an orange skirt, so I bought the yellow one instead.
*Did that make you anxious?*
No.
*... Melissa.*
First-world issues.
*You're being sarcastic again.*
I call it humor.

Conversation with my therapist when I was 16.
That was my last time seeing her.

# Scene 69

*Setting: Pool deck*
*Chapter: One-month-therapy*

*So, what's new?*
Um… nothing.
*Okay... how are you feeling today?*
Fine.
*Just fine?*
Yep.
*For a writer, you don't have that much to say.*
I know that.
*Do you want me to get you a pen and paper? Maybe that will help.*
No.
*Is someone making you come here?*
Obviously, I'm 17. I'd rather do anything but sit my ass in yet another therapist's office.
*What else would you rather do?*
Read.
*Maybe instead of avoiding your problems by reading about other peoples' problems, you should fix yours first.*
I'm here because I can't fix my issues, and people think that talking to some random person with a degree is going to fix it instantly.
*I know you're going through a lot, but you're being a little aggressive.*
You haven't seen me aggressive. You don't know me.
*Yet I could tell that you read to silence your issues. I'm here to help you fix that.*
If you're going to shit on me because I read, then I'm leaving.
*Then get out.*

<u>I get up from the chair to leave the room.</u>

*That's another issue, Melissa. You're so used to being left that now you always have to be the one that leaves first.*
Who are you to say that to me?
*I have your files here. I know how many therapists you've spoken to.*
Because they leave.
*And now you're trying to leave because you don't want to be left.*
…
*It's okay to be upset because of that, but I'm here to stay.*
I leave for graduation in a few months.
*That's a whole few months to sit here and tell me how you feel. So, sit back down and stop being sarcastic.*

<u>I sat down, and we talked.</u>

# Scene 70

*Setting: Pool office*
*Chapter: Green-eyed poet*

Do you remember
How in that one poem
I said,
*"I would rather feel everything than nothing."*
Yeah...
Although that is true,
I curse myself for that.
I feel too deeply,
I look into people too deeply,
Then I hurt myself over it.
I tell myself over and over,
*"I will not fall for him. I will not."*
But I fucking do.
It's like the poet in me.
Needs to feel deeply.
Has to care about people
And God forbid a special someone
Enters my life.
Falling deep into a pool of the
Green eyes of a guy who
Writes poetry.
A guy who seems to like me
As much as I like him,
Which quite honestly scares the crap
Out of me.
I always liked people more than they
Liked me.
I know that's not a good thing,
But I bring it up because
I'm struggling to wrap my head around
The fact that someone *likes* me,

Knowing that I think deeply about everything.
This isn't a sob story.
This is me trying to piece together-
This is me trying to piece myself together
To learn how to accept someone
Liking me
Without me being insecure about it.

# Scene 71

*Setting: Pool deck*
*Chapter: Green Eyes*

I used to love brown eyes
Because of the warmth it gave me
When they looked into mine.
I used to like blue eyes
Because I loved to swim in them.
Now,
I'm trapped in his green eyes
And I can't help but love
Getting lost in forests now.

# Scene 72

*Setting:* Bedroom
*Chapter:* Trainwreck

When will I fucking learn?
I've been through so many heartbreaks
That I don't know what to do anymore.
It's the same thing over and over again.
I get my heart broken.
I fix myself.
Like another guy.
Rinse and repeat.
Nobody is made to like or love me,
Just me.
As I said before…
I'm too confusing,
Too emotional,
Too bitchy,
Too raw.
But don't feel bad for me:
That's just how it is.
Call it whatever you want but
I don't expect anyone to put
Up with my bipolar bullshit,
And good luck with trying to get me
To open up.
My books are the only thing
That knows the truth,
And the truth is…
I *really* like this green-eyed boy.
I like the way he talks,
Laughs,
Listens,
Writes,
Smiles,

Everything.
But I'm scared to fuck it up.
I'm scared of being too complicated,
And being too much to handle.
So,
I sit here and down a vodka cooler,
Feeling my heart speed,
And hoping that I don't fuck it up.
Hoping that, for once, I'll
Be able to open up and
Realize that maybe
I didn't have anything to be afraid
Of, after all.

# Scene 73

*Setting: Pool deck*
*Chapter: Kind of girl*

My therapist always told me.
To stop apologizing for who I am,
But I can't help it and
Do you know why?
I'm not the kind of person to
Be friends with or date.
Honestly,
I'm quite boring.
I read, write, take care of my pets,
Work, study, and drink.
I like road trips and
Always being on-the-go.
That's as exciting as I'm going to get.
I'm not the kind of girl who
Parties every weekend.
(My European parents would *flip*)
I'm not the kind of girl who
Takes eddies and wanders the streets
Of Toronto.
I'm not the kind of girl
You pick me up at 12 in the morning.
I'm not the kind of girl who has casual sex.
I'm not the kind of girl who smokes.
I'm not the kind of girl you call
When you want to have a wild time.
I'm the kind of girl you call
When you're crying.
I'm the kind of girl who has to
Be home by 10:30 pm.
I'm the kind of girl to pull all-nighters…
To read.

I'm the kind of girl who shows up to
Work or school
Half an hour early.
The kind of girl that people my age call
Boring.
What's hard about being this kind of girl
Is never being fun enough,
Risky enough,
Wild enough for someone my age to like.
I know what all the adults are
Going to say,
*"Melissa, it's okay. In the future, you're going to be the girl that a guy wants to settle down with."*
Although it's great for a guy to want to
Settle down with me,
What about now?
I'm going to be boring until I turn 27.
I'm going to have a lineup of guys
Wanting to settle after years of being
With the wild girls?
No,
Because I wasn't enough for them before,
So why now?
I don't want to be enough as soon
As he wants to settle down.
I want to always be enough.

# Scene 74

*Setting: Bedroom*
*Chapter: Don't say*

Please don't say
That you love me.
I heard that lie way too many times.
I'd rather you just say that
You like me
Than give me false hope.
I know that I'm not a very lovable
Person.
I mean,
I could be nice and
Treat the people that I love
Very special…
But I'm also
Moody.
Bitchy.
Bipolar.
Anxious.
Quiet.
Raw.
Loving me is loving a poet.
A rollercoaster of emotions
That I 99.9% of the time
Refuse to tell anyone.
Someone who looks deeply
Into everything.
Please don't say that you love me.
It's not possible.

# Scene 75

*Setting: Sheridan*
*Chapter: Bitch*

A lot of people ask me
Why do I call myself a bitch?
Do I actually think that
I'm a bitch?
Sometimes.
That's not the point though.
The point of calling myself
A bitch is that
Other people who dislike me
Are going to call me a bitch anyway.
So why not beat them to the punch?
The answer to why I
Call myself a bitch is quite simple:
It softens the blow.

# Scene 76

*Setting: Bedroom*
*Chapter: I'm Not a Good Girlfriend*

I will love you.
I will care about you.
I will try my best to treat you right,
But I'm a shitty girlfriend.
I'm insecure-
Extremely insecure.
I get flashbacks of the
Ghost of his hands on me,
And I panic.
I'm jealous.
I will compare myself to
Every girl you've ever liked.
You could call me
Beautiful and smart,
But I'll still compare myself
Because I self-sabotage.
I get panic attacks,
Having to down prescribed clonazepam
That makes me look like a
Drug addict for 3 days straight.
I can't fucking eat without
Feeling guilt and shame.
I'm really fucking annoying,
Especially when I'm stubborn.
I'm afraid of love.
Nobody will ever love me as a whole.
I know that for a fact.
I'm okay with that fact or
At least trying to be.
Yes,
I write beautiful poetry but

That is because the inside of me
Is so ugly,
And I try to at least make it
Presentable through my poetry.
Some days
I wake up already wanting to
Give up,
But I don't.
I'm a terrible girlfriend
Because I can't accept
Somebody loving me whole.
No matter the reassurance,
I don't accept it.
It's not for me.

# Scene 77

*Setting: Bedroom*
*Chapter: 3 main characters*

Meet the 3 main characters in my mind.
Meet Love.
She's always thinking about
Her green-eyed boy,
Always wanting to hug him,
Talk to him,
Be with him.
Always thinking about him.
His curly brown hair,
As she runs her fingers through it.
His amazing cinnamon scent.
The happiness she feels when
She's with him.
The alive,
Care-free and happy girl.
Meet Insecurity.
She is always arguing with Love,
Calling Love a
*"Love-blind fool."*
Insecure spends her time looking
In the mirror with a marker,
Drawing circles around the places she wants
To lose weight.
She thinks,
*"Once I lose that, I will be pretty."*
But nothing is ever good enough,
Because she always thinks that there
Are a few more pounds to lose.
Everyone gets annoyed with Insecurity.
When Insecurity and Love argue,
It's never good.

*"He loves you!"*
Screams Love.
*"I'm not enough!"*
Screams Insecurity.
Insecurity knows that he will leave her
If she continues being a mess,
Yet she doesn't know how to stop.
She drinks to get her mind off
Everything once in a while.
Love gets annoyed with that.
*"Alcohol is unhealthy. You're killing yourself."*
Love says.
*"It's better than being a drug like you, Love. I may be unhealthy and annoying, but you're literally an addict."*
Insecurity snaps.
That is when the third character,
Reality,
Comes in.
Reality is logical.
She grabs Love by the throat and
Lectures her about the dangers of
Being too love-blind.
Then,
Reality pins Insecurity down and
Tells her that nobody likes a
Self-pitying bitch.
Welcome to the inside of my head.

# Scene 78

*Setting: Pool deck*
*Chapter: Baba*

This poem is dedicated to
My baba.
I love her so fucking much.
She is always there for me.
Most of my childhood memories
Have her in them.
She is my best friend,
Alongside my mom.
She teaches me Croatian,
Teaches me about my Croatian family history,
She tells me stories,
She listens to me.
I feel like if I didn't have her with me,
I'd be lost.
I don't know who the fuck I am
Without her.
When I say that she is everything to me,
I mean it.
I love her more than she'll ever know.

# Scene 79

*Setting: Pool deck*
*Chapter: Poet in Love*

You know
I'm serious about you
Once I write poetry
About you.

# Scene 80

*Setting: Pool deck*
*Chapter: My subconscious belief*

My supervisor
Once asked me a question.
*"Melissa, why do you shut yourself out to everyone?"*
A million reasons ran through my head,
But I didn't admit any of them.
I shrugged my shoulders in response.
So,
Why do I shut myself out from everyone?
The truth is
That I don't want to hurt other people,
And I don't want to get hurt.
By keeping myself at arm's length
It means that nobody is close enough
To hurt me,
And I'm not close enough to hurt them.
Growing up,
I've always wanted to travel the world.
Going from place-to-place.
Always being on the go.
Then,
I read a self-help book
When I was 16.
It stated that my desire
To travel alone was connected
To my subconscious belief
That I didn't want to get too close
To anyone,
Because then they could abandon me.
My desire to travel alone
Meant that I'd make friends
With people from different places,

Keep them at arm's length,
Then leave.
Leave before they could leave me.
Leave before they get too close.
So I guess that my answer to that question
Is this poem.

www.ingramcontent.com/pod-product-compliance
Lightning Source LLC
Chambersburg PA
CBHW072213070526
44585CB00015B/1317